The Kids Laugh Challenge

Would You Rather?

St. Patrick's Edition

Funny Scenarios, Wacky Choices and Hilarious Situations for Kids and Family

With Fun Illustrations

RIDDLELAND

Table of Contents

Introduction   pg 5

Rules of the Challenge   pg 7

Would You Rather?   pg 9

Did you enjoy the book?   pg 108

Bonus Book   pg 109

Contest   pg 110

Other books by Riddleland   pg 111

About Riddleland   pg 114

Riddleland Bonus Book

Join our **Facebook Group**
at **Riddleland for Kids** to get
daily jokes and riddles.

http://pixelfy.me/riddlelandbonus

Thank you for buying this book. We would like to share a special bonus as a token of appreciation. It is a collection of 50 original jokes, riddles, and two super funny stories.

Introduction

"A good friend is like a leaf clover semi-colon hard to find and lucky to have." ~ **Unknown**

We would like to personally thank you for purchasing this book. **Would You Rather? St Patrick's Edition** is a collection of the funniest scenarios, wacky choices, and hilarious situations for kids and adults to choose from.

These questions are an excellent way to get a conversation started in a fun and exciting way. Also, by asking "Why?" after a "Would you rather" question, you may find interesting answers and learn a lot about a person.

We wrote this book because we want children to be encouraged to read more, think, and grow. As parents, we know that when children play games and learn, they are being educated while having so much fun that they don't even realize they're learning and developing valuable life skills. 'Would you Rather ...' is one of our favorite games to play as a family. Some of the 'would you rather ...' scenarios have had us in fits of giggles, others have generated reactions such as: "Eeeeeeuuugh, that's gross!" and yet others still really make us think and reflect and consider our decisions.

Besides having fun, playing the game also has other benefits such as:

- **Communication** – This game helps children to interact, read aloud, and listen to others. It's a great way to connect. It's a fun way for parents to get their children interacting with them without a formal, awkward conversation. The game can also help to get to know someone better and learn about their likes, dislikes, and values.

- **Builds Confidence** - Children get used to pronouncing vocabulary, asking questions and it helps to deal with shyness.

- **Develops Critical Thinking** – It helps children to defend and justify the rationale for their choices and can generate discussions and debates. Parents playing this game with young children can give them prompting questions about their answers to help them reach logical and sensible decisions.

- **Improves Vocabulary** – Children will be introduced to new words in the questions, and the context of them will help them remember them because the game is fun.

- **Encourages Equality and Diversity** – Considering other people's answers, even if they differ from your own, is important for respect, equality, diversity, tolerance, acceptance, and inclusivity. Some questions may get children to think about options available to them, that don't fall into gendered stereotypes, i.e., careers or activities that challenge the norm.

Would You Rather?
St. Patrick's Edition

How do you play?

At least two players are needed to play this game. Face your opponent and decide who is **Lucky Leprechaun 1** and **Lucky Leprechaun 2**. If you have 3 or 4 players, you can decide which players belong to **Lucky Leprechaun Group 1** and **Lucky Leprechaun Group 2**. The goal of the game is to score points by making the other players laugh. The first player to a score of 10 points is the **Round Champion**.

What are the rules?

Lucky Leprechaun 1 starts first. Read the questions aloud and choose an answer. The same player will then explain why they chose the answer in the silliest and wackiest way possible. If the reason makes the Lucky Leprechaun 2 laugh, then Lucky Leprechaun 1 scores a funny point. Take turns going back and forth and write down the score.

How do you get started?

Flip a coin. The Lucky Leprechaun that guesses it correctly starts first.

Bonus Tip: Making funny voices, silly dance moves or wacky facial expression will make your opponent laugh!

Most Importantly: Remember to have fun and enjoy the game!

8

Would You Rather...

Spend a whole month searching for a pot
of gold at the end of every rainbow you
see but never find the gold OR spend
ten years searching for a pot of gold
and finally find it?

Find a pot of gold that brings you only
bad luck but still leaves you rich OR find a
four-leaf clover that has no value other than
bringing you luck every day of your life?

Would You Rather...

Wear a top hat that's too big and keeps falling over your eyes OR wear a pair of plaid green pants that are one size too small?

Live in a leprechaun's home cozied up inside a log OR spend a day hiding in the bottom of a pot of gold so you can surprise the leprechaun owner?

Would You Rather...

Gold coins fly out of your mouth every time you laugh OR have four-leafed clovers sprouting out from between your toes?

Go frolicking with a mermaid in the ocean waves and find a shiny pearl OR dance with a leprechaun to get a coin from his pot of gold?

Would You Rather...

Gold coins pop out of your couch cushions every time you sit down to watch TV OR find dollars stuck between the pages of every book you read?

Play tic-tac-toe using gold coins with a leprechaun OR play a game of chess with a board that has only leprechauns as pieces instead of bishops, rooks, kings, queens, and knights?

Would You Rather...

Grow a lucky rabbit's foot out of one of your legs OR find a lucky penny in your belly button every time you get dressed?

Your best friend is a leprechaun who has an anger management problem OR have a pet unicorn who likes to poke things with its glittery golden horn?

Would You Rather...

Eat a whole pot of chocolate coins wrapped in golden foil OR drink a giant blender full of mint chocolate chip milkshake in one hour?

Go to Ireland, the land 'o the Irish, for a week and have it rain the whole time OR meet a leprechaun and then lose your sight for a week because you weren't supposed to see the leprechaun?

Would You Rather...

Leave a trail of gold coins behind you with every step but not be able to pick up the coins OR have a big pot of coins all to yourself that's really heavy and hard to carry?

Give a super lucky four-leaf clover to your worst enemy OR to your least favorite sibling?

Would You Rather...

Win the lottery and find out you are being paid in stuffed animals OR find a pot of gold at the end of the rainbow and find out that you can't take it away from the rainbow or it will turn into sand?

Live the luckiest day of your life as a kid OR save your luckiest day for the future when you're a grownup?

Would You Rather...

Find a pot of gold coins that you can spend on anything you can buy in a store OR find a magic lamp with a genie inside and be granted three wishes about anything at all, imaginary or true?

Attend a St. Patrick's Day party where all the food and drink are green OR a party where none of the food is green but somehow it turns your lips and tongue green?

Would You Rather...

Wear green from head to toe - green shoes, socks, pants, shirt, hat OR have all your skin painted green from your feet all the way to your forehead for a whole day?

Square dance with a bunch of friends in a big red barn OR be known for doing an Irish jig while wearing all plaid clothes?

Would You Rather...

Wake up to find your hair has turned as green as a bunch of spinach OR wake up to find that your hair has turned into pure shiny gold?

Have something amazing happen that never should have happened and never happens again to you OR work really really hard to make something amazing happen that can happen again because you've worked so hard?

Would You Rather...

Give the pot of gold that you find at the end of the rainbow to your favorite volunteer organization, like to help get pets adopted OR take gold coins to people in your neighborhood who you know could use a little help?

Kiss a big warty toad for good luck OR capture all the black cats in the world to prevent one from giving you bad luck?

Would You Rather...

Get paid a gold coin every time you clean your messiest sibling's room OR get paid one gold coin after doing dishes and cleaning up the messy kitchen in your house for a whole week?

Have the power to grant wishes to anyone in the world OR have the power to give someone good luck which doesn't mean they'll get what they want?

Would You Rather...

Be best friends with a leprechaun and not be able to tell anyone or he'll go away forever OR secretly be a leprechaun but not be able to tell anyone or show anyone your pot of gold because it'll disappear forever?

Play a game of chess after finding a lucky penny and defeat a chess master using luck OR play a masterful game of chess strategy and win with your talent?

Would You Rather...

Be the luckiest person in the world always getting everything you want and having everything go your way OR the smartest person in the world who can solve any problem and always knows more than everyone in the room?

Live a very planned-out life where every thing happens just like you want it to OR live a very lucky life where unexpected and cool things randomly happen to you?

Would You Rather...

Eat a bowl of smelly green cabbage soup OR take a bath in a tub full of warm smelly cabbage soup?

Have enough luck to make everything turn out okay in the end OR have enough happiness that you're never really sad but never really joyful either?

Would You Rather...

Spend a day playing at a playground made of rainbows you can climb and slide down OR race around a gold coin-covered playground trying to gather more coins than your friends?

Be spelled by a wizard and able to cast small spells of your own OR be granted lifelong good luck by a leprechaun at the end of the rainbow?

Would You Rather...

Catch the Easter Bunny and force him to give you all his chocolate and candies OR catch a leprechaun and force him to give you his pot of gold and good luck?

Get a lucky penny by biting into it while eating a chocolate sprinkled donut OR while eating a bowl full of chocolate chip mint flavored ice cream?

Would You Rather...

Find a lucky penny and then step on your own finger OR step on the tail of a black cat and then find a $20 bill?

Win an arm-wrestling contest against a muscular leprechaun dressed all in green OR against a very plump and hearty-looking Santa Claus?

Would You Rather...

Eat ice cream made from green tea mixed with cream OR eat tangy key lime pie for dessert for the rest of your life?

Trade in all your luck for a one-time large cash payment OR purchase luck on an as-needed basis for small amounts of cash throughout your life?

Would You Rather...

Trade the thing you love most in the world for the luckiest rabbit's foot ever OR trade all your future luck for a pot of gold?

Have a giant piggy bank full of coins that weighs five pounds OR have a wallet or purse full of dollar bills that weighs one pound?

Riddleland

Would You Rather...

...rainbow going right over your head ...ver you go OR randomly have gold coins appear in your shoes?

Always know the right answer to every question you are asked, no matter what the topic is OR be able to build anything out of any material that you are given?

Would You Rather...

Find a lucky $1 bill on your pillowcase each night OR find your favorite thing to eat for breakfast on your table each morning?

Be incredibly lucky every single day for a whole year OR be on an incredibly bad streak of luck for one whole week and then have pretty good luck for two years straight?

Would You Rather...

Your hands turn into four-leaf clovers,
so you'd no longer have a thumb to grab
things with OR your feet turn into miniature
rainbows, so you'd no longer have toes?

Get your head stuck in a pot of gold that
you found OR try to discover where
unicorns live?

Would You Rather...

Be lucky enough to always have a job that makes you enough money OR always have a refrigerator that has just enough of your favorite food?

Be the lucky charm for someone else who always wants to be around you OR be able to get your luck from one of your friends but only when you are around him or her?

Would You Rather...

Carry a tiny little leprechaun in your pocket OR wear a big old necklace with a large rabbit's foot around your neck for good luck?

Speak with an Irish accent for three days and have no one be able to understand what you say OR hear everything that everyone around you says in an Irish accent and not be able to understand what they say?

Would You Rather...

Eat only green colored food like spinach,
lettuce, Brussels sprouts, and green beans
OR eat your regular diet of foods but
have everything taste like mint for
one whole month?

Find thick sticky green earwax in your ears
OR gooey green eye boogers in your eyes on
St. Patrick's Day?

Would You Rather...

Dye your hair bright green for St. Patrick's Day and not be able to wash the dye out of your hair for a week OR paint your finger and toenails green and have your fingernails stained green for a month?

Eat a breakfast in bed of green eggs and ham OR eat supper in front of the TV of stuffed cabbage and corned beef?

Would You Rather...

Deep clean your house and find gold coins instead of dust bunnies under all the furniture OR live in a house that is filled with completely green colored furniture?

Wear green pajamas with four-leaf clovers all over them to bed each night for a year OR go out in public wearing a full leprechaun costume on St. Patrick's Day?

Would You Rather...

Sleep on a pillow that smells like your favorite peppermint candy OR go to sleep with green cucumber slices over your eyes?

Dance a lively Irish jig with every step you take for a week OR only talk in rhyming limericks for a month?

Would You Rather...

Wear big black buckled shoes like a leprechaun every day OR have pointy elf ears like a leprechaun?

Have the high-pitched elf-like voice of a leprechaun OR be unusually short like a leprechaun?

Would You Rather...

Spend two hours looking for a four-leaf clover in a field of clovers OR spend two hours trying to make a perfect four-leaf clover out of green construction paper using glue but no scissors?

Be the child of the luckiest parents in the world OR be the sibling of the luckiest brother or sister in the world?

Would You Rather...

Wear checkered pants to school every day for a year OR wear a big green top hat with a big black and gold buckle on it to school every day for a month?

Spend a month researching about the country of Ireland OR spend a week learning how to sing a bunch of traditional Irish folk songs?

41

Would You Rather...

Find money in your grandma's old purse that smells like mothballs OR find money in your grandpa's old hat that smells like sweat and fish?

Eat all your food covered in squirts of golden mustard OR covered in drizzles of thick green minty syrup?

Would You Rather...

Wear a pair of really ugly green eyeglasses every day OR have neon green eyes that glow in the dark?

Spend an afternoon hiding real golden coins for someone else to find OR spend an afternoon putting up signs for a St. Patrick's Day scavenger hunt?

Would You Rather...

Have to cheer up a grumpy leprechaun in order to earn his pot of gold OR have to learn a leprechaun's dance in order to earn his pot of gold?

Eat a sandwich made with bread that is not moldy but tastes moldy OR with bread that is green and moldy but tastes just fine?

Would You Rather...

Find a pot of gold at the end of the rainbow and have to pay money to get it OR help a leprechaun style his hair in order to get the pot of gold?

Get every assignment from your teacher written in riddle form OR have to write all the answers on all your assignments in riddle form?

Would You Rather...

Wear a leprechaun costume every day for a week after St. Patrick's Day OR sing loudly, "Top O' the day to ye" every time you enter a room?

Prove that leprechauns are real and know where real pots of gold are located OR prove that unicorns with magical horns and sparkly manes that look really cool but don't do very much are real?

Would You Rather...

Adopt a cute little leprechaun as the youngest sibling in your family OR be adopted as the largest and oldest sibling into a leprechaun's family?

Only be able to see the color green OR see everything in rainbows?

Would You Rather...

Dive into and swim in a pool full of thick green lime flavored jello OR eat green pistachio pudding all day on St. Patrick's Day?

Travel all the way to Ireland to Blarney Castle so you can kiss the Blarney Stone OR would you rather have someone just tell you what the Blarney Stone was and save you the trouble?

Would You Rather...

Have green grass growing on top of your head that needs to be cut weekly like your lawn OR have a bright green tongue with green mossy stuff on it every morning that grows overnight?

Play a traditional Irish folk song using a pipe OR play an Irish folk song with your bow and fiddle?

Would You Rather...

Eat a supper of boiled potatoes and mashed peas OR eat a supper of green potato chips?

Learn about traditional Irish meals such as boiled cabbage OR read a comic book with a leprechaun as the main character?

Would You Rather...

Play hide and seek with a tiny leprechaun who is really hard to find OR try to find a needle in a haystack?

Swim in a giant pool filled with heavy golden coins OR dive into a giant pool of creamed potato soup?

Would You Rather...

See your reflection as a leprechaun every time you look into a mirror OR smell nothing but mint every time you sniff with your nose?

Be an Irish potato farmer during the Great Potato Famine and be very hungry OR guard an Irish castle on rainy days without an umbrella or raincoat?

Would You Rather...

Trade your dad out for a leprechaun OR trade your brother or sister out for a leprechaun?

Your face turns green every time you get embarrassed OR that you cry green tears every time you are sad?

Would You Rather...

Cut out 100 four-leaf clovers out of green construction paper OR apply green glitter to 100 four-leaf clover cutouts with a bottle of glue?

Have eyelashes like the brightest green Irish emeralds OR have teeth that are the freshest shade of green grass?

Would You Rather...

Live with a BFF leprechaun who is always playing pranks on you OR with a BFF leprechaun who is always singing and dancing to Irish music?

Be granted three wishes by a leprechaun whom you've captured OR steal the leprechaun's pot of gold from the end of the rainbow?

Would You Rather...

Be a leprechaun who oddly has very bad luck OR be a leprechaun who has the problem of always being broke (i.e., having no gold in your pot)?

Have your name announced when you enter a room with an O' before it so it'd become like O'Tom or O'Madison OR do a little jump and click your heels together every time you leave the room?

Would You Rather...

Trade pants with a leprechaun for a day
OR trade shoes with a leprechaun
for one day?

Travel to Ireland by plane and lose your
return ticket home while in Ireland
OR travel to Ireland by boat and get
shipwrecked on the island?

Would You Rather...

Run across a rainbow to get to school every day OR have a real castle to play in at your school playground?

Have a crayon box filled with only green crayons OR have a pencil box filled with only green colored pencils?

Would You Rather...

Go through a pot of gold coins, biting each one with your teeth to make sure it's real OR find a pot of gold that has a map with twenty clues leading to a different treasure?

Wear green lip balm OR put green colored hair gel in your hair every day for a week straight?

Would You Rather...

Make a leprechaun hat to wear on St. Patrick's Day out of construction paper and glue OR make a leprechaun hat out of popsicle sticks glued together and colored with green markers?

Celebrate your birthday on St. Patrick's Day and have a green birthday cake every year OR celebrate St. Patrick's Day with a traditional meal of artificially colored green food every year?

60

Would You Rather...

Have green colored lights in your classroom at school OR have green colored lights in your bathroom at home?

Walk barefoot through a field of four-leaf clovers, squishing them with every step you take OR walk under a giant row of ladders and see if you get bad luck?

Would You Rather...

Only be able to speak in tongue twisters that leave your mouth and your brain exhausted OR finish every sentence by saying "Kiss me, I'm Irish"?

Be the only person wearing pink from head to toe at a St. Patrick's Day parade OR show up to a Halloween party dressed as a leprechaun?

Would You Rather...

A leprechaun sneaks into your house and messes it all up OR a leprechaun sneaks into your classroom and messes it all up?

Wear a royal crown made of deep green emerald stones OR a crown made of pure blue sapphire stones?

Would You Rather...

Be able to move around without making
a single sound so no one notices you OR
have Irish music playing in the background
every time you get up from your seat
and walk around?

Have a big smear of red juicy ketchup
on your cheek OR have a small but very
visible piece of green spinach stuck in
your teeth all day?

Would You Rather...

See shamrocks every time you close your eyes OR have rainbows fly out of your mouth every time that you laugh?

Find a friend wherever you go in the world OR take the same friend with you wherever you go in the world?

Would You Rather...

Have the bright red hair that many Irish people are known for OR be able to change your hair color just by thinking about it?

Have one perfect shamrock OR ten shamrocks that look like something nibbled on each of them for luck?

Would You Rather...

Paint four-leaf clovers all over the walls of your room OR hang giant hand-painted cardboard fourleaf clovers all over your bedroom ceiling?

Eat a pound of cabbage in one sitting OR a small plateful of cabbage at each meal for a month?

Would You Rather...

Design a trap to catch a leprechaun OR sew a tiny outfit made especially for a leprechaun?

Only be able to see the color green on St. Patrick's Day every year OR always see everything in green on all other days of the year?

Would You Rather...

Keep a pot of gold all to yourself and not be able to spend it OR give all the coins from a pot of gold to your friends?

Take a week-long trip to Ireland in five years OR spend five hours in Ireland right now?

Would You Rather...

Wear a pair of green socks that leave your feet green OR a pair of green mittens that leave your hands green?

Trade places with a leprechaun and sit around waiting near the end of a rainbow OR trade places with the tooth fairy and spend every night of your life flying around collecting childrens' lost teeth?

Would You Rather...

Take a bath in a tub full of shelled green peas OR play in the pool using giant green beans as pool noodles?

Be in charge of bringing green colored treats for the class St. Patrick's Day party OR be in charge of designing costumes for the class President's Day play?

Would You Rather...

Use a green toothpaste that leaves your teeth a nasty moldy green color OR that leaves them bright white but makes your mouth smell like moldy bread?

Stand under a double rainbow OR stand in the middle of a tall field of green grass?

Would You Rather...

Pay a gold coin every time you need to use the toilet OR pay a gold coin every time you want to open your refrigerator?

A mischievous leprechaun switches everyone's desks in your classroom OR a mischievous leprechaun breaks every single pencil and uses up every eraser in your classroom?

Would You Rather...

Open your mouth and see a tongue that
is as green as a snake OR open your mouth
and see a tongue that is as colorful as
a rainbow?

Have the luck of the Irish only one day
per year for the rest of your life OR
have the luck of the Irish any day of your
life that you wear all green clothing?

Would You Rather...

Sleep inside a pot of gold instead of in your comfy cozy bed at home OR sleep in your own bed which has gold coins shoved in random places underneath your mattress like the Princess and the Pea story?

Only be able to grow flowers that are the color green OR only be able to eat food that is the color green?

Would You Rather...

Be stuck outside in a rainstorm of showering green raindrops OR a blizzard of delicate green snowflakes?

Set up an evergreen tree covered with shamrock ornaments every year for St. Patrick's Day OR dye a basket of all green Easter eggs for Easter?

Would You Rather...

Drive in a car that has only green tinted windows OR live in a house where every window is tinted Green?

Chew minty green bubblegum for twenty-four hours straight OR suck on one mint candy per hour every hour for two days?

Would You Rather...

Wake up and have traditional leprechaun colors - green, black, and gold streaks in your hair OR wake up and have hair that has turned a bright carrot orange color?

Watch TV on a screen that only shows the color green OR play a video game on a screen that is completely green?

78

Would You Rather...

Appear green in every photo you take OR have the background of every photo you are in appear green?

Eat a bowl of macaroni and cheese that is dyed green but tastes yummy OR eat a bowl of beautifully orange and cheesy looking macaroni and cheese that tastes like broccoli?

Would You Rather...

Wear a green uniform to work every day OR wear green pajamas to bed every night?

Wake up covered in green spots that are ugly but don't bother you OR wake up covered in red itchy spots all over your body?

Would You Rather...

Be sung an Irish lullaby by your mom or dad every night before you go to sleep OR wake up to a lively Irish song on your alarm clock every morning?

Do all of your schoolwork on a computer screen that is broken and only shows the color green OR do all of your schoolwork on green construction paper using only a green marker or colored pencil to write with?

Would You Rather...

Get green colored braces put on your teeth at the orthodontist OR wear a pair of neon green framed eyeglasses?

Have your family benefit from your little brother or sister capturing a leprechaun and all his good luck OR have your class benefit from your teacher capturing a leprechaun and all his good luck?

Would You Rather...

All your family's dishes come out of the dishwasher green OR all your family's clothes come out of the laundry green on St. Patrick's Day?

Pay for your good luck by having one unlucky thing happen to you for every lucky thing that happens OR pay for your good luck by having to do one extra chore for every good thing that happens to you?

Would You Rather...

Find a lucky penny with your face on it OR find a lucky penny with your favorite celebrity's face on it?

Count your blessings by literally putting a tally mark on a notebook you carry with you everywhere OR mark your blessings by saying "Hallelujah!" every time something good happens?

84

Would You Rather...

Grow lucky four-leaf clovers out of your armpits OR have a lucky four-leaf clover stuck to the middle of your back where you can't reach it?

Be an artist who can only create beautiful works of art that are pure green OR live in a city where there are only green buildings and houses?

Would You Rather...

Be lucky during the hours of 8pm to 8am every day OR be lucky only on Mondays every week?

Smell minty fresh green soap wherever you go OR smell like you just rolled around in a field of fourleafed clovers?

Would You Rather...

Be lucky every day of the year except for your birthday OR only be lucky on one day - your birthday - but then you're super lucky that day?

Live in a place where the sky is always a shade of emerald green OR where the clouds always look like puffs of minty green cotton candy?

Would You Rather...

Be so lucky that you get things just by thinking about them OR get your luck by writing everything you want out on a sticky note?

Be unable to hear anything at all OR only be able to hear the sound of an Irish fiddle?

Would You Rather...

Be super lucky only when you're playing video games by yourself with no witnesses OR make beautiful works of art that only look beautiful in your eyes?

Dump a big minty green St. Patrick's Day milkshake on the head of anyone you choose OR chug a giant minty green St. Patrick's Day milkshake in less than five minutes?

Would You Rather...

One of your eyes could only see the color green OR one of your lips turned green while the other stayed Pink?

Sprout the orange-red hair of a leprechaun from between your toes OR sprout clumps of orange-red leprechaun hair from the knuckles on your hands?

Would You Rather...

Open your mouth to reveal a tongue
covered with bright green glitter OR
leave trails of green glitter falling
out of your hair wherever you go?

Begin every sentence with "that reminds
me of when I was in Ireland" OR end every
sentence with "what happens in Ireland
stays in Ireland"?

Would You Rather...

Wear a big green hoodie that is always hanging over your face OR a pair of big green sweatpants that are always falling down?

A leprechaun be in every story that you write during writer's workshop in school OR have a leprechaun be a character in every single book or story that you read?

Would You Rather...

Trade your favorite toy for a pot of gold that you can't see how many coins are in it OR trade your favorite toy for the privilege of being able to slide down a rainbow whenever you want?

Play a game of leapfrog with two leprechauns having them try to jump over you OR double Dutch jump rope with two leprechauns swinging the jump rope for you?

Would You Rather...

Leave green fingerprints on everything you touch OR leak bright green drool droplets out of your mouth whenever you eat?

Spend a year going to school in Ireland without any of your friends or teacher OR have a new student from Ireland join your class and sit in the seat right next to you?

Would You Rather...

Read a book of 200 Would You Rather questions that are only about leprechauns OR write 200 Would You Rather questions only about leprechauns?

Spend the winter in a place where it's snowy all of the time and the snow is always an odd green color OR live on a beautiful island where the sun always shines green?

Would You Rather...

Stream online music where every station and playlist is Irish music OR take Irish fiddle lessons three times a week?

Get an illness that can only be cured by eating tons of green leafy vegetables OR have a skin rash that can only be cured by applying green pea baby food all over your body?

Would You Rather...

Receive shamrocks for every birthday
and other present that you get for a whole
year OR receive all your gifts wrapped in
the same shamrock wrapping paper every
single time (it never goes away)?

Your teacher writes on the white board
with only green markers OR your school
cafeteria serves only green food on
St. Patrick's Day?

Would You Rather...

Be lucky enough to have clean smelling and looking clothes without ever having to wash them OR be lucky enough to have clean smelling and looking teeth without ever having to brush them?

Trade hair with a red bushy-haired leprechaun OR have all the hair fall off your head mysteriously one day?

Would You Rather...

Spend Christmas with a Santa Claus dressed in a green suit from head to toe OR spend St. Patrick's Day with a leprechaun who speaks with an Irish accent but says "ho ho ho" in every sentence?

Get lost in an old abandoned Irish castle that is rumored to be haunted OR spend an afternoon shopping in a mall that is blasting traditional Irish folk songs?

Would You Rather...

Bleed green when you fall and scrape your knee on the sidewalk OR blow green snot out of your nose all the time during allergy season?

Spend your weekend doing good deeds for others that make you feel really good about yourself OR spend the weekend getting random gifts from friends that are really thoughtful and kind?

Riddleland

Would You Rather...

Be able to play any ball sport you want during recess, but all the balls have turned green OR have a swimming pool in your backyard all summer long, but the water is always green?

Be able to sink the winning half-court basketball shot by pure luck OR spend an hour each day practicing so you can sink that same shot by pure skill?

Would You Rather...

Spend six hours trying to teach a leprechaun how to play video games OR spend two hours listening to a leprechaun tell you a scary story about mean fairies?

Be really really lucky but in order to do so you have to have a bright green shamrock tattooed on your forehead OR only be lucky when you wear your t-shirt that has a big green shamrock on the front of it?

Would You Rather...

Turn into a rich leprechaun but never be able to leave your pot of gold at the end of the rainbow OR not have a lot of money but pretty good luck?

Go to a school where every floor, including the gym, is colored bright green OR go to a school where every ceiling in each room is painted bright green, including the cafeteria?

Would You Rather...

Say the word "luck" instead of "love", so you'd say "I luck it" instead of "I love it" OR end every sentence by saying "lucky duck"?

Your cheeks turn a minty shade of green whenever you're embarrassed OR your eyes turn an intense shade of green whenever you're angry?

Would You Rather...

Find earwax-covered gold coins in your
ears OR booger-covered gold coins
in your nose?

Drink all your sodas with green ice cubes
in them that color the sodas green OR
bite into a piece of buttered toast without
seeing the big patch of green mold on it?

Would You Rather...

We all carry around golden coins instead
of paper money in our wallets and purses
OR we all carry around big black pots
where we keep our paper money
and coins?

St. Patrick's Day was a school holiday
so no school on that day each year OR
that Valentine's Day was a school holiday
with no school on it?

Would You Rather...

Play outside in mint-green snow that tastes like mint ice cream OR find five gold foil-wrapped chocolate coins in your backpack each school day?

Be the only leprechaun in your family who doesn't have orangey-red hair OR be the only leprechaun in your family who is over three feet tall?

Did you enjoy the book?

If you did, we are ecstatic. If not, please write your complaint to us and we will ensure to fix it.

If you're feeling generous, there is something important that you can help me with – tell other people that you enjoyed the book.

Ask a grown-up to write about it on Amazon. When they do, more people will find out about the book. It also lets Amazon know that we are making kids around the world laugh. Even a few words and ratings would go a long way.

If you have any ideas or jokes that you think are super funny, please let us know. We would love to hear from you. Our email address is - **riddleland@riddlelandforkids.com**

Riddleland Bonus Book

Join our **Facebook Group**
at **Riddleland for Kids** to get
daily jokes and riddles.

http://pixelfy.me/riddlelandbonus

Thank you for buying this book. We would like to share a
special bonus as a token of appreciation. It is a collection
of 50 original jokes, riddles, and two super funny stories.

Would you like your jokes and riddles to be featured in our next book?

We are having a contest to see who are the smartest or funniest boys and girls in the world! :
  1) **Creative and Challenging Riddles**
  2) **Tickle Your Funny Bone Contest**

Parents, please email us your child's "original" Riddle or Joke and **he or she could win a $25 Amazon gift card and be featured in our next book.**

Here are the rules:
  1) We're looking for super challenging riddles and extra funny jokes.
  2) Jokes and riddles MUST be 100% original—NOT something discovered on the Internet.
  3) You can submit both a joke and a riddle because they are two separate contests.
  4) Don't get help from your parents—unless they're as funny as you are.
  5) Winners will be announced via email or our Facebook group – Riddleland for Kids
  6) In your entry, please confirm which book you purchased.
  7) Email us at Riddleland@riddlelandforkids.com

Other Fun Children Books for Kids!

Riddles Series

The Laugh Challenge Series

Would You Rather... Series

Get them on Amazon
or our website at www.riddlelandforkids.com

About Riddleland

Riddleland is a mom + dad run publishing company. We are passionate about creating fun and innovative books to help children develop their reading skills and fall in love with reading. If you have suggestions for us or want to work with us, shoot us an email at riddleland@riddlelandforkids.com

Our family's favorite quote:

"Creativity is an area in which younger people have a tremendous advantage since they have an endearing habit of always questioning past wisdom and authority."
~ Bill Hewlett